EDINBURGH IN FOCUS

EDINBURGH IN FOCUS

PHOTOGRAPHY BY MARIUS ALEXANDER

TEXT BY NEIL MACLEAN

HarperCollins*Publishers*

HarperCollins Publishers
PO Box, Glasgow G4 0NB

First Published 1992

ISBN 0 00 435648 9

Reprint 9 8 7 6 5 4 3 2 1 0

A catalogue record for this book is available from the British Library.

Printed in Hong Kong

Contents

Introduction

This is a book about Edinburgh. It is not a guide book to the city; it would not help anyone find the modern art gallery or Edinburgh Zoo or the best Italian restaurant in the Old Town. Nor, although it dips into Edinburgh's past, is it a history book tracing the steps of Bonnie Prince Charlie or the dates of Mons Meg or marking the spot where Rizzio fell. It is just a book about Edinburgh, images in words and pictures, as much for the people who live here as for those who have left or those who are just passing through.

The views are personal and inevitably ambivalent. Edinburgh is unquestionably one of the best cities in which to live (it is reputed to have the best quality of life in Britain), but there are also uncomfortable sights to be seen, wherever you point your lens or pen. It is part of our heritage to have mixed feelings about where we live: a close affinity to the land, a frustration with the parochial, a great affection for the people, a sadness at so little ambition in their bones.

It is a familiar theme in Scottish literature but these are also real feelings shared by many who live in Edinburgh: those who have seen the St James Centre rise in place of Georgian terraces, who have seen a hole in the ground grow weeds where they could have watched operas, who see the desolation of Wester Hailes, Muirhouse and Craigmillar, who live in the AIDS capital of Europe, who live in one of the most beautiful cities in the world.

While commentators from outside might see just a castle and an embarrassment of riches, it would be dishonest of those living here not to acknowledge that there are also people stopping you for money beside the Mound, drugs for sale in shopping centres, that the beach at Portobello has lost its appeal (and, besides, the sea would leave a very nasty taste in your mouth if you were unlucky enough to drink it), and that a mean spirit peeks behind so many net curtains and through so many Georgian letterboxes. Yet, that having been acknowledged (explaining why the views in this book are not all rosy-hued), we can then celebrate the city with a clearer conscience.

In this book there are scenes taken from contemporary Edinburgh life – a day on the Royal Mile, a winter's morning in the New Town, a walk along Edinburgh's coast on the last day of summer, May Day on Arthur's Seat, the strange life of the Festival Fringe – moments which might strike a chord in the heart of anyone who knows the city well, even if it is years since they last climbed the Camera Obscura, had coffee in Jenners or walked through the Hermitage of Braid. For if this book is looking to provoke any emotion at all (and what book does not?), it is that tiny extra pulse of recognition, the thrill of the familiar.

Neil MacLean 1992

Lawnmarket close

I

The Old Town

'Now – can everybody see?' She looks round at the little faces, straining for a better view. 'All right. Well, this camera was installed in 1853 by an Edinburgh optician called Maria Theresa Short and was later taken over by the town planner and sociologist, Sir Patrick Geddes.' It is like an incubator in the Camera Obscura, a warm orange light glows on the children waiting to see what is going to unfold. They shriek as she turns the lights out. 'Please miss, can we play Murder in the Dark?' And then Edinburgh appears, in a perfect circle before them, filling the edges of a drum like a witch's cauldron. They gasp. 'Can you see the little people moving about down there?' Small hands stretch out to disturb the 'water'. 'We can do a trick here.' She slides a piece of paper onto the screen and, raising the paper, seems to lift a man, a woman and a child from the High Street as if they were walking across a magic carpet.

From above, on a clear winter's day, the Old Town looks as gaunt and bare as a skeleton. Over the years the curved spine of the High Street has been picked clean of its puffy flesh; the overcrowded, unsanitary lands have gone, the black labyrinth has been dismantled, Edinburgh's washing has been taken in. But there is still life in the old bones yet. 'And what is that up there?' She wheels her periscope. 'That's right – it's Edinburgh Castle. Now, have you all visited the castle...?'

I leaned over the ramparts by St Margaret's Chapel above the cemetery where they buried the officers' dogs, while the children clambered over the cannons, imagining a bloody war on Princes Street below. It was five to one, lunchtime, and a tense expectant hush fell all around us. On a barked command, Tam the Gun, the District Gunner, stamped up in his shiny number one dress uniform, the garb of a sergeant of the Royal Artillery. He loaded the old Second World War field gun, stamped around a bit more, then stared intensely at the stopwatch in his hand. Five, four, three – the children screwed up their faces, some covered their ears, others braced themselves against the wall – two, one; he pulled the lever. Nothing happened. Birds sang, cars hooted on the street below, dogs barked in the High Street, but on the ramparts of Edinburgh Castle, nothing happened. We were there on The Day The One O'Clock Gun Misfired. 'Somebody will be in big trouble now,' said the attendant at the door of the chapel. A woman giggled nervously. 'He could at least have shouted bang,' said a man with a German camcorder and a waxed moustache. Slowly the crowd dispersed, and the children climbed down from their canons.

In her flat in Ramsay Gardens – 'Garden, please. Allan Ramsay only had one garden' – Elizabeth

Mason, as precise as a stopwatch, dusted her 17th-century rosewood cabinet and rearranged her flowers. 'It used to shatter our windows, you know. I've got cracks in the corner of my windows caused by that gun.' She looked through her dining room window at the castle. 'And living here during the Tattoo is no joke either, I can tell you; one can hardly get to one's door. The tourists can't imagine anyone could possibly want to go up the hill when they are all coming down.'

But, for many people, Ramsay Garden is the most coveted of Edinburgh addresses; a picturesque block of flats, with red roofs and apple white walls high above Princes Street. It was built by Sir Patrick Geddes around the octagonal 'goose-pie' house of the poet Allan Ramsay as accommodation for students, placed next to the castle to show that 'even the poor can relate to the mighty'. 'And you know,' she said peering at me through the thick lenses of her spectacles, 'it's far less up-market and far less wealthy than everyone supposes. We're mainly retired professional people here now; although there's been a lot of trouble in the past when the wrong sort of people have moved in. There was one lady who had a chain of sweetie shops. She was just awful; she had no manners. She finally left saying she was not welcome here. Well, she was right – she wasn't.'

There is a plaque on the reservoir by Ramsay Garden, the source of the Old Town's first piped water supply, commemorating the burning of witches on Castle Hill; more than three hundred between 1479 and 1722. Edinburgh was a centre of witchcraft in Scotland. When a woman was suspected of being a witch, she was tried by the city's magistrates who would stick her with needles and strip her to the waist to see if Satan had 'nipped her person'. It was an expensive business, disposing of witches in those days. According to Presbytery records in 1633, it cost £3.6s.8d for enough wood to burn just one witch – about £3.33 in today's money.

'That'll be £2.50 for the adults and £2 for senior citizens,' said the woman at the door of the Scotch Whisky Heritage Centre, formerly Castlehill School. Inside, two Spanish girls stood in a model of a washback. 'Eemageen zees is full of wort,' one of them read from the panel. 'Please,' she said to me, 'what ees thees word – wort?' The frothy malt above us looked like a giant pizza and sounded like a grim primeval swamp. 'It's a sort of swampy pizza,' I said, helpfully, and they wrote that down in their notebooks. Upstairs, in a darkened film set, we sat in a large, whisky barrel-shaped invalid car and slid through the history of the dram. A taped commentary gabbled from between our knees, hens clucked in a plastic midden and the smells of pine bonfires smouldered in our nostrils. Someone, I noticed, had looped a pair of mirrored shades round a waxwork model of Rabbie Burns. 'O Whisky! soul o' plays an' pranks! Accept a Bardie's gratefu' thanks!' In front of us, a Japanese businessman snored gently in his plastic barrel.

But the centre is a harmless tourist trap, picking dollars and yen from visitors' wallets on their way down from the castle, the first step on a heritage trail that will show them exactly what they had always hoped to see and, therefore, the best-selling view of Scotland. There is nothing wrong with that: give them what they want and they will come back for more. But truly to see ourselves as others see us is to go shopping along the High Street – Hector the Haggis, lucky grouse claws, Nessie eggs, Greyfriars Bobby tea towels and polyester tartan panties – and to blush at our own reflection in the shopwindow 'mirror'.

Across the street, the periscope turns above its tower. 'Now this church – does anyone know its name? Who said St Giles? Wrong, Catriona. This is St John's Highland Kirk; Gaelic services used to be held here. It's also the highest point in Edinburgh. The highest but not the tallest. It stands at 241 feet, so high we can't even see the top of it, no matter how hard I try to tilt my mirror.' They swivelled their heads as she tried to tilt her mirror. 'Now we're looking down The Royal Mile which goes all the way down to Holyrood Palace. But although it's called The Royal Mile, it's actually a mile and an eighth, which is an old Scots mile.'

Down below, a figure halts under the statue of Walter Francis Montagu Douglas Scott, 5th Duke of Buccleuch and 7th Duke of Queensberry, and spits carefully onto the road. The 'Heart of Midlothian', outlined on the cobbles, marks the site of an old and hated prison. Tradition has it that that is why so many locals spit on it, although Hibernian football fans are more likely to spit on it because it also happens to be the badge of their local rivals, Hearts. The dour grey face of St Giles looms above them ('heavy is the kirk that wears the crown'). Properly known as the High Kirk of Edinburgh, it is a place of contradiction, rather like the city itself: Church of Scotland but with an Anglican style, where angels play bagpipes but John Knox taps his bible solemnly above the pews (and we know what that means). And while the congregation celebrates communion on a Sunday morning, the smell of rich Scotch broth drifts up from the Lower Aisle.

William Macaulay looks like God – except he is probably smaller and his long white beard is stained yellow from smoking his favourite pipe. Every morning he sits on the public benches in the High Court in Parliament Square by St Giles, reaching forward to see better, cupping his ear to hear justice being done. 'Everybody must do their bit, you see,' he says. Besides, it is the best free entertainment in the city. Better, he declares, than the Sheriff Court across the road. 'It's full of rabble, and the lawyers are such a scruffy bunch.' 'The court will rise,' says the usher. His Lordship bows to the court, Macaulay bows to the judge. The clock has stopped at a quarter to three and here before us are all the caricatures of the Scottish legal system: the irascible and eccentric judge in his silks, peering sternly at a pale and nervous defendant, while the advocate with his thumbs in his dandruffed waistcoat stands in front of the jury denouncing the wretched man. 'One advocate used to keep a silver matchbox at the end of his watchchain,' Macaulay slides along the bench to whisper. 'He used to show off to the jury by swinging it on his chain while he was summing up. My, but I'll never forget the day the matchbox burst into flames.' And he sniggers into his copy of *The Scotsman*. Below, the lawyers scribbling at the table under their white and curly wigs look just like sheep grazing.

Opposite St Giles, in a fine panelled room in the City Chambers and under the portraits of late and famous provosts, Edinburgh District Council's housing sub-committee discusses their tenants' rent arrears; another free show and just as well-rehearsed: unemployment, poverty and government policies from one side, 'scroungers buying video recorders instead of paying their rent' from the other. And they all vote as ever, stuck in the tram lines of party rhetoric.

'And that,' she says pointing to a spire, 'is the Tron Church. They used to keep the public scales, known as the Salt Tron, there and if anybody was caught trying to cheat, they used to nail their ears to the weigh beam.' The children make noises of disgust. 'Please miss, my brother got a policeman's hat there once.' It is the most pagan of Edinburgh's rituals; to gather by the Tron at Hogmanay and kiss strangers on the stroke of midnight, when a Caledonian Cinderella transforms herself into Mr. Hyde.

Further down the Royal Mile, a line of schoolchildren files slowly through the tall glass doors into the Museum of Childhood. Nobody has told their teacher it is not for children. 'This is not a museum for children, it is about them,' said Joseph Murray when he opened it in 1955. And it is for their parents and anyone else who remembers malt and cod liver oil and Five Boys chocolate and Barratt's Sherbert Fountain. Not for the little children, with their noses pressed against the panes, gazing wistfully through the windows – looking out.

Out of sight of the Outlook Tower, there is life in the old burgh of the Canongate where the Old Town still wags its tail. There are real people living there and children playing in the school, students at the college, and grocers and a fish shop and a bank. In Jenny Ha's, Betty still sits at the end of the bar with a nip of whisky and the old men from next door still complain when their glasses are half empty (when really they're all half full). One of Edinburgh's hidden treasures lies close by in Dunbar's Close: a small plot of paths and sweet-smelling herbs, laid out in the style of a 17th-century Edinburgh garden with neat squares of Lilliputian hedges. It is a supremely peaceful place to sit in the sun. Very few people know about it and few visitors waver from the well-worn path down to Holyrood.

'And here we are back at the castle,' she says, as the periscope swings back to where it started. 'Well, I hope you all enjoyed yourselves.' They all cheer 'yes', except for a little girl with pigtails and bright yellow raincoat, who has come with her father all the way from Glasgow. Her face is the picture of disappointment. She expected greater things from the witch's cauldron. 'Aw daddy,' she protests, 'is that a' we're gonnae see – just Edinbra?' And he takes her to the shop to buy some sweeties.

The Old Town overlooking Princes Street Gardens (above)
Ramsay Garden (right)
Old Town sunset (opposite)

Ramsay Garden details (above and opposite)

The Royal Mile (right and opposite)

Coffee
House

Canongate Tolbooth museum, Royal Mile (right and opposite, top)

White Horse Close, Royal Mile (opposite, bottom)

Kinloch Anderson

John Knox's House, Royal Mile (opposite and top left)
Gladstone's Land, Royal Mile (top right and bottom)

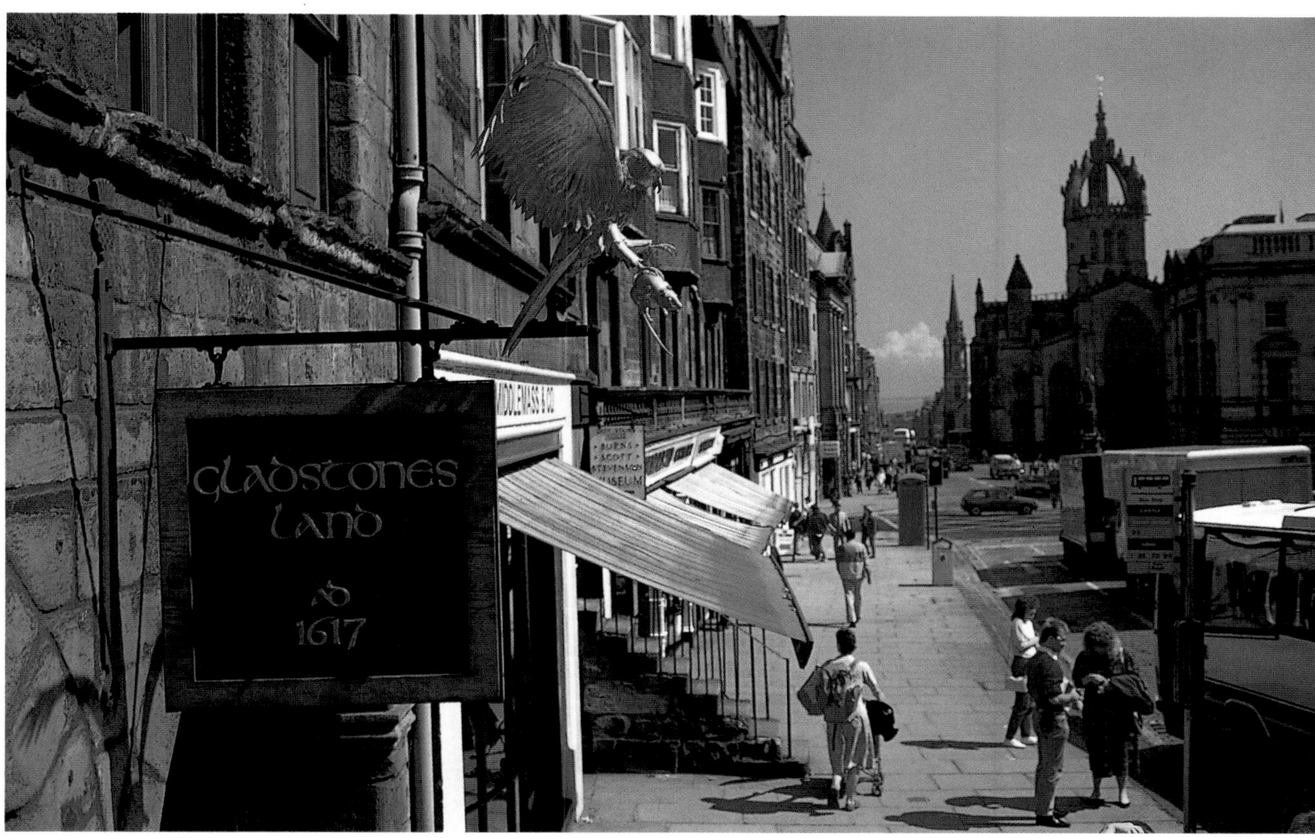

HOUSE OF
KILTMAKING
KNITWEAR

Celtic
Craft
Centre
KILT
OUTFIT
£180.

Lawnmarket close (top left)
Holyrood Abbey carving (bottom left)
Lady Stair's House museum (right)
Royal Mile kiltmakers (opposite, top left and right)
Oddfellow's Hall (opposite, top centre)
High Street close (opposite, bottom)

Richard Demarco, local gallery owner and patron of the arts (top)

Old Town shop signs (bottom)

Hogmanay crowds at the Tron Church, High Street

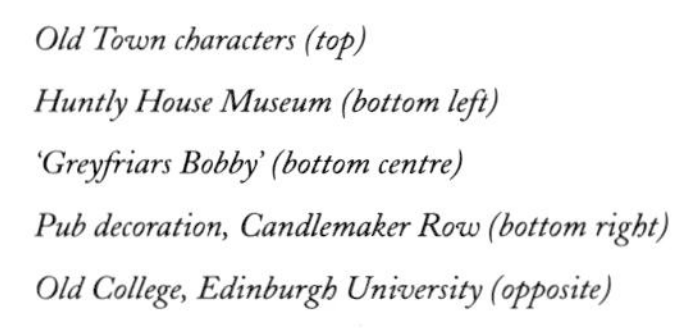

Old Town characters (top)
Huntly House Museum (bottom left)
'Greyfriars Bobby' (bottom centre)
Pub decoration, Candlemaker Row (bottom right)
Old College, Edinburgh University (opposite)

The Old Town by night (top)
Free Church Assembly Rooms (bottom left)
High Street carving (bottom right)

Museum of Childhood (top)
Huntly House Museum (bottom)

TENNENT'S
LAGER

Doorway, St Mary's Episcopal Cathedral (top)
'Heart of Midlothian', High Street (bottom)
St Giles Cathedral, High Street (opposite)

Palace of Holyroodhouse

Parliament Square

The Palace of Holyroodhouse

The Mound (top)
Preachers, The Mound precinct (bottom)

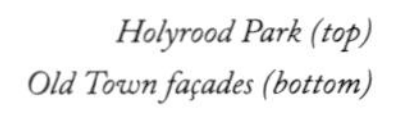

Holyrood Park (top)
Old Town façades (bottom)

The Grassmarket (top)
Edinburgh Castle (bottom)

Edinburgh Castle

Statue of George IV, George Street

2

The New Town

They sound like a flock of starlings; the ladies with hats. Each morning they gather in Jenners department store, in the restaurant, with its views across Princes Street to Edinburgh Castle, Ramsay Garden, New College and the wedge in the middle of the Scott Monument (like a Gothic spaceship with booster rockets) to fall on cream fancies, caramel wafers or 'just a plain biscuit and a cup of tea', to rest their feet and exercise their tongues. Like a flock of starlings. 'And of course, I said to Robin, you can't expect the Council to do it for you, not now these Labour people are in,' and she carves a scone into narrow bite-size pieces.

The hats are functional: fur – they may not sell fur any more in Jenners but you can still wear it there with pride – or knitted bonnets tightly piped around their skulls, or deerstalkers for hunting woollies and a casserole in Marks and Spencer. Early photographs of Princes Street hang around the walls above them. In them, the grandmothers of these same women stride businesslike between the trams and carriages. It was a confident place at the turn of the century: the trees are smaller, but the road is broader and Princes Street seems a much grander boulevard.

The City Fathers nearly built on both sides of the street. Fortunately, that idea was abandoned, because it is the open side of Princes Street, where it is no street at all, where it drops to Princes Street Gardens to give an unobstructed view of the castle on its rock, that makes it one of the greatest streets in Europe. If they had built there, if that was now a mirror image of the shops and concrete façades on its northern side, it would hardly be remarkable. John Ruskin once said Princes Street had as much beauty as a cabbage stalk. If they had built on the southern side, he would have been completely right and the view from Jenners, from above the plates of shortbread, would have been of fast food or just another Mothercare.

She pats her lips with her (still folded) napkin. 'I must get something for Robin's tea. I thought perhaps beef olives would be nice' and she marches off through the Food Hall, her shoes as sensible as a fixed-rate savings account, to glare at *bouchées feuilletées* (reduced) and traditional Scots black bun, her hat like a pelmet round her head.

But you need a hat in Edinburgh, on the days when the east wind slaps your ears and pokes your eyes; on the clear shopping days on Princes Street when your breath leaves clouds against the pale blue sky. I left the crowds one morning and walked up Hanover Street, past the imposing and ugly façade of the Trustee Savings Bank and, by the great green dome of the Commercial Union, crossed the street to stand under the statue of George IV on his royal roundabout. To the south lay the castle, the spires of New College, the solid Doric façade of the Royal Scottish Academy and, behind it, the slopes of the Mound (built from New Town building rubble). By the Mound lies Princes Street Gardens, where Robert Louis Stevenson once sniffed the air. 'It is what Paris ought to be,' he wrote. And it was. Perhaps it still is. If Paris were more like Princes Street, Parisians would not be quite so rude (cold, yes, but not so rude) and there would be a lot less public kissing on the Champs Elysées.

In the Gardens, spreadeagled against a ladder under the turbanned statue of Allan Ramsay, Jimmy Ford was planting bulbs in the floral clock: echavaria, cressola, sygenia, lobelia. 'It's hard work but it's worth it,' he said, to see the tourists' admiration throughout the summer. 'Hey, is that the floral watch?' say the Americans, nodding at the 8-foot-high minute hand, waiting for the cuckoo. One summer, a cat waited for the cuckoo every day.

To the north, beyond the trees at the edge of the city, lay the blue ribbon of the Firth of Forth and, beyond this, the green hills of Fife. On either side, to the east and west, crowded the manic jumble of architectural styles which makes up George Street.

George Street was the true axis of the first New Town, designed by James Craig who won the competition to design the city's new extension. Narrow lanes were built for shops on either side, Rose Street and Thistle Street, while Princes Street and Queen Street were residential streets beyond. The great squares, Charlotte Square and St Andrew Square, weighed in on either side. Craig was surely a man who kept his pencils in a neat row between the ink pots on his desk. George Street is a chocolate box of buildings; Italian Renaissance, Doric, Corinthian, Glaswegian Edwardian, Baroque; palaces, churches and banks, with domes and spires and columns and great bay-windowed façades.

The Assembly Rooms were opened on the 11th of January 1787 with a glittering ball. At 92 feet long and 42 feet broad, the Assembly Room itself was reputed to be 'the largest room in Britain except the Great Room at Bath' and 'it is said to exceed that in elegance'. It was the centre of the social scene in the New Town. Dickens read there, Turner painted there, Chopin played there, and it was renowned for its dancing assemblies. It still is. Every second Wednesday during the winter months, Phyllis Drummond and her friend Janet attend a tea dance at the Assembly Rooms. 'The Tommy Mitchell Trio play the dances – they're the best. He keeps a strict tempo does Tommy Mitchell, not like some younger ones.' And they dance *Cheek to Cheek*, *Satin Doll*, *Steppin' Out* and *Anything Goes*. They always dance together. 'There are two women for every man. And I tell you, there's a lot of fit-looking men.' Between dances, they sip their tea and eat buttered scones. They are friendly affairs, the tea dances. 'When one old dear couldn't remember where she'd put her handbag, we had a whip-round and she went away with ten times more than what she came with.'

Between Queen Street and the second New Town, lie Queen Street Gardens, acres of bordered lawns and neatly planted flower beds to which the general public have no access whatsoever. On winter mornings it is an eerie experience to stare over the spiked barricades or the barbed wire above the gates, squinting into the low sun against the thick barrier of trees and holly onto the deserted lawns and empty paths. Stevenson found inspiration here for *Treasure Island*, but for most of Edinburgh, it is *The Forbidden Planet*. The residents of houses nearby hold the keys to Queen Street Gardens but most days, you will hardly see anyone there unless it is a solitary dogwalker, who seems so unreal in this forbidding landscape, it is like a ghost figure in a children's story. It is surely time they were opened to the public.

Lady Dunpark has a different view. She looks

down onto the gardens from Stevenson's old bedroom in Heriot Row. 'I'll tell you what, my dear,' she says in her soft Irish brogue, 'if we opened the gardens, the vandals would just take the place over. You know we've just spent a couple of thousand pounds just on the trees. Besides,' – and she prodded me gently on the arm – 'it's not just the wishes of the people here; it would take an Act of Parliament to make these gardens public.' She lent me the key and, as the heavy gate clanged shut behind me, the gardens seemed like the loneliest place in Edinburgh.

The streets of the northern New Town – Heriot Row, Abercromby Place, Drummond Place and Great King Street – are seldom busy. Their grand and elegant, but strictly disciplined, façades hardly encourage idle strollers. This may be the most extensive Georgian development in Europe, but you do not hear Edinburgh folk say, 'let's take a walk around the New Town' on a Sunday afternoon. With each house a triple arms-length from the pavement, behind javelin railings, and across a bridge above the street, it is hard to see or even imagine life behind these windows. Great King Street on a Saturday can seem a bleak and draughty place, with its closed societies and lawyer's dens and 'period offices', with a single bouquet of bright balloons tied to the railings for a child's birthday party looking as out of place as a barber's pole on a Wee Free church.

The New Town slips smoothly down to Stockbridge (someone once suggested the only difference between the two was that the Stockbridge entrance stairs have more of a tendency to smell of cats than those further up the hill) and St Stephen's Street, by William Playfair's tall, square-built, heavily-knuckled church, is the hyphen between the two. In his light museum, Mr Purves, thickly bearded under his three-ringed hat, leans against a cat's head cane, and polishes an old gas mantle. 'Gas was the thing in the New Town,' he says, peering at me above his glasses. 'While London was just building bits of a city, we built the whole city and there was a great deal of money around then to embellish the buildings with the very latest thing. And the very latest thing was gas.' He pauses to smooth his kilt around his knees. 'But the old gas fittings were scrapped for their brass during the war and anyway, they became an undesirable feature in the houses, nobody wanted them.' A straggle of customers shuffle between the shelves, between the piles of paraffin lamps and rolls of flex, looking for period pieces while trying to duck the heavy fittings hanging from the ceiling. 'Have you got a shade for this?' asks a little man holding a nude Art Deco lamp by the lady's ankles. For a light museum, it seems a very dark place.

The shops are busy in Stockbridge. The charity shops and the shops selling lentils and monkfish tails and aromatherapy oils and the Astrology Centre ('you don't have to be psychic to work here but it helps') with its star charts for personal organisers and natal interpretations. I bought a horoscope –'Someone understands how you feel and is sympathetic today' – and a tape of the music of flowers.

In Inverleith Park by the pond, men are sailing model boats. Big men with little boats, as serious as a power cut in the City, clumsy beside the swans. At the edge, a boy in a green anorak watches as his cabin cruiser sinks slowly in the middle of the pond. And still watches, long after his ship has gone. In the playing fields above him, older boys are playing for their schools; rugby for the posh schools, football for the comprehensives. In Edinburgh, your school is the caste mark on your forehead. It is the Edinburgh question: what school did you go to? Answer it, and your past hangs out behind you like a shirt tail and expectation dangles awkwardly before your eyes. Across the road, the Academy is playing Stewarts Melville, watched by a line of fathers in Barbour jackets and corduroy trousers. 'Come on the Academy,' they shout, as steam rises from a heaving scrum of first-years. 'Pull him down now Hamish.' Hamish, who has been eating grass all morning, squares up to Goliath and bites the turf again.

In the Botanic Gardens nearby, young couples push strollers along the paths while their toddlers chase pigeons between the neatly labelled trees. Now and then a squirrel darts towards them looking for food. It is a pleasant place. Above the Arboretum, a lady with a small brown hat sits on a bench and stares at the city's skyline over the trees; to the hills, the castle, to the neat Georgian terraces, to the city spires. And what spires. In Princes Street, by the Royal Scottish Academy, there is a model of Edinburgh for the blind. If you close your eyes and run your hand across the shapes, you have a view of Edinburgh of sorts. But it is a blunt impression. If the spires were right, I swear you would cut your fingers to bloody shreds. I look at her again, but she is fast asleep.

Inverleith Park (above)
Old Observatory, Calton Hill (opposite, top)
Princes Street (opposite, bottom left)
George Street architecture (opposite, bottom right)

89

Tea dance, Assembly Rooms, George Street (top)
George Street sign (bottom left)
Calton Hill (bottom right)
Princes Street Gardens (opposite, top)
Calton Hill (opposite, bottom)

North Bridge and the Balmoral Hotel (top)
Dean Village (bottom)
Monument to Dugald Stewart, Calton Hill (opposite, top left)
Princes Street Gardens (opposite, top right)
National Monument, Calton Hill (opposite, bottom)

Georgian architecture, Moray Place (above)
Charlotte Square (left)
New Town panorama (opposite, top left)
Princes Street Gardens (opposite, centre left)
Pub sign, West Register Street (opposite, top right)
Calton Hill by night (opposite, bottom)

The
GUILD
FORD
Arms

Princes Street rush hour (top right)
The Royal High School, proposed venue for a devolved or independent Scottish Parliament (bottom right)
New Town doorway (below)

George Street (top)
Charlotte Square (bottom)

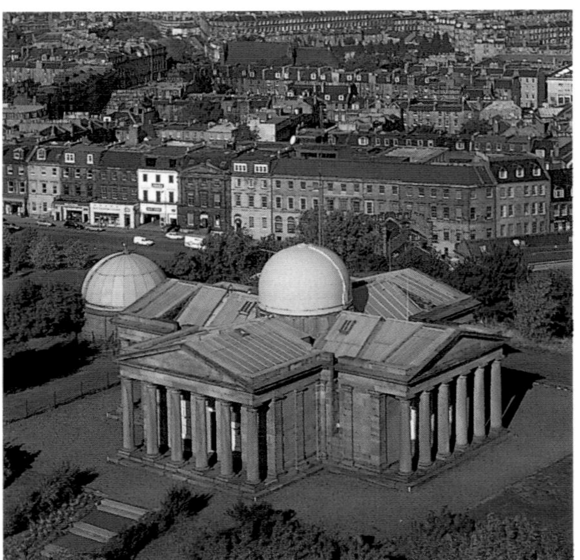

Morning tea, Jenners Restaurant (top)
New Observatory, Calton Hill (bottom right)
Waterloo Place (bottom left)
New Town doorway (opposite, top left)
Statue of Sir Walter Scott (opposite, top right)
Floral clock, Princes Street Gardens (opposite, bottom)

EVENTY
FTH ANNIVERSARY
1985

Princes Street (top)
Stockbridge (bottom)
War memorial, North Bridge (opposite, top)
Heriot Row façade (opposite, bottom left)

St Andrew's and St George's Church, George Street (top right)

Georgian façade, Atholl Crescent (top left)

St Andrew House (bottom)

Queen Victoria, Royal Scottish Academy (top)
Royal Bank of Scotland, St Andrew Square (bottom)

ANCHORA
SALUTIS

Edinburgh Academy rugby (top)
Princes Street Gardens (bottom left)
Mr Purves, Purves Lighting Emporium, Stockbridge (bottom right)
Hanover Street detail (opposite, top)
Princes Street Gardens (opposite, bottom)

St Bernard's Well, Stockbridge (below)
Georgian windows (opposite, top)
Inverleith pond (opposite, bottom)

The Scott Monument, Princes Street (above)

Fettes College, Comely Bank (opposite)

Royal Botanic Gardens
National Monument, Calton Hill (opposite, top right)
St Mary's Episcopal Cathedral (opposite, top left)
St Andrew Square (opposite, bottom)

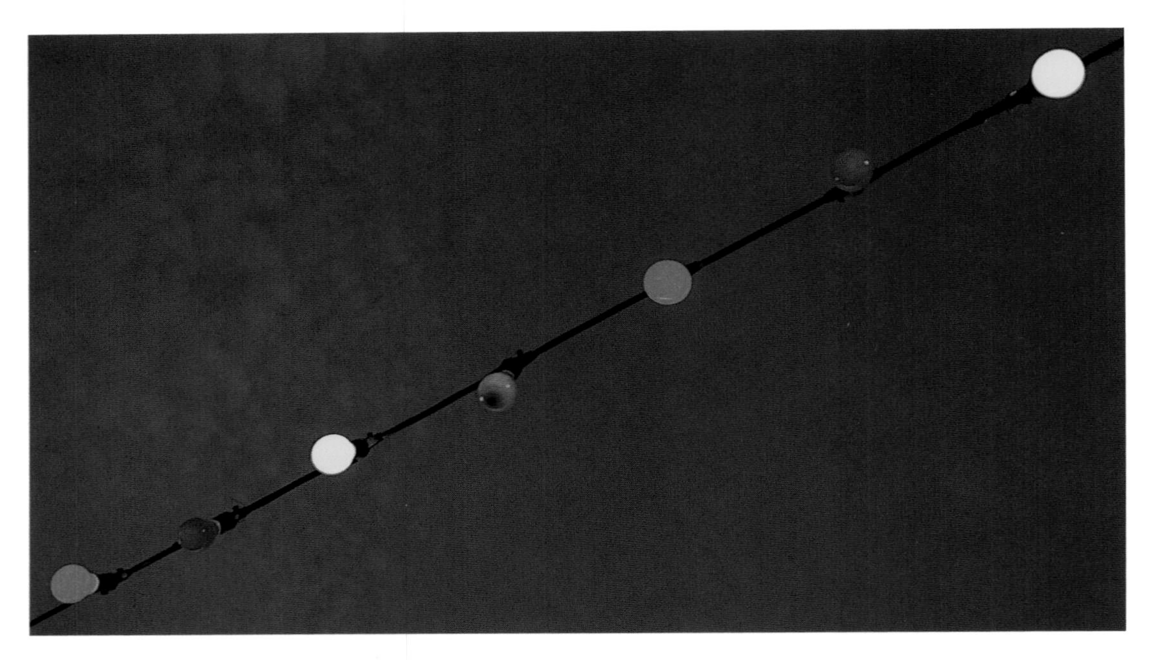

Festival lights

The Festival

Titania yawned. 'What angel wakes me from my flowery bed?' It was Yasmin, aged two-and-a-half, wearing a large yellow wig and singing *Ten Green Bottles* at the top of her voice as she picked her way through the sleeping cast of *A Midsummer-night's Dream*. It can be hard to find somewhere to stay in Edinburgh when the city becomes the biggest top to the biggest arts circus in the world and for the amateur thespians of Ipswich School, home was an old youth club annexed to a children's nursery on the north side of the city.

Oberon had got up early, disturbed by Peaseblossom's snoring and by his habit of grinding his teeth loudly in his sleep. Scratching, Oberon surveyed the dozing mass of humanity camped across the youth club floor: one of the sprites, over-canopied with luscious woodbine or at least moth-eaten blankets, was sleeping between the faded tram lines of a badminton square, still wearing her fairy costume (inside out). Oberon wanted a shower – there was something nasty in his hair – but the little children were in the toilets learning how to brush their teeth and he could not face the noise. They would be out soon, stamping their way through the hall, hand in hand, singing 'If you're happy and you know it clap your hands' or something just as bad. God, his head hurt.

He focused on the faded signs above the basketball nets: 'No man is fully educated who cannot adjust himself to the circumstances in which he finds himself. No chewing gum is allowed on these premises.' If only they hadn't gone on to the Fringe Club last night. If only he hadn't eaten that chicken curry. He looked at the yellowing wallpaper in the tiny kitchenette they shared with 15 kayaks and a roof rack. If only they had stayed in Ipswich.

The cause of his misery started, if only he knew it, back in 1947. The war was over, austerity prevailed and Edinburgh decided to establish herself as a culture capital of the world. 'She will surrender herself to the visitors,' said the Lord Provost, Sir John Falkoner, 'and hopes that they will find in all the performances, a sense of peace and inspiration with which to refresh their souls and reaffirm their belief in things other than material.' And they did. They came in droves, paid the ticket prices and their belief in things other than material soared, thanks to Kathleen Ferrier singing like a linnet and Bruno Walter's baton. In that same year, the reels rolled for the first time on the Film Festival and not long afterwards, the first Military Tattoo upset the residents of Ramsay Garden. But it was when the Fringe came skidding onto the stage on the coat tails of the official Festival that Edinburgh in August started to become seriously silly. Add the jazz, the book, and the television festivals and what Sir Thomas Beecham once called a very nice affair turned into a bodice-ripping romance with Bohemia. For some at least.

Reaction to the Festival is mixed; for many Edinburgh people, it is not just a waste of time but a positive nuisance – the city's walls are covered with posters, you cannot walk down a city-centre street without someone playing a tin whistle in your ear looking for money, Princes Street is jammed solid with tourists, car parking is even more impossible than usual and just try driving up The Mound after the Tattoo has disgorged its tartan and gabardined hordes. Some find it a source of mystery. Late one night the telephone rang in the Festival office. It was a little old lady wanting the times of the buses to Moffat. 'Why are you phoning here?' they asked. 'Because I looked in the telephone book and you were at the top of the list of useful numbers.'

Other people from Edinburgh welcome this annual distraction – the sight of their dowdy city loosening her stays – while remaining strictly on the periphery of events. They buy tickets for the occasional big name attraction, line the streets for the Festival Parade and the Jazz Parade, and flood into Queen's Park for Fringe Sunday to learn to juggle, to watch their children's faces being painted and to see the kites fly over Arthur's Seat, all the while avoiding anything too suspiciously arty. But many people plunge headlong into the three-week jamboree, spending hours poring over the programmes, planning their days, trying to see as many shows as possible in 24 hours, doing alien things like eating their dinner after eight o'clock at night, dancing in the street, being nice to the Scientologists on the South Bridge and going to the Traverse Theatre on a Monday evening. It may be an international festival but most of the bottoms on the seats come from Edinburgh.

At her desk in the Fringe office, juggling the demands of 500 companies, 1,000 shows, 9,000 performances and a small packet of cheese and smoked ham sandwiches from the Italian delicatessen, Mhairi Mackenzie-Robinson was not alarmed to see a man on stilts suddenly appear outside her first-floor window. It had happened every day that week and, anyway, he was useful for conveying messages down below. There was the usual commotion on the street outside, from Fringe groups advertising their shows and performing for the public in the queue for tickets. A prim-looking woman was playing Saint-Saëns on a saw; a man, only just dressed in wrestler's trunks, was standing on the old stone plinth in a position that could only cause him pain; a pantomime zebra was haranguing a critic he had recognised from last year's show; and, somewhere a few yards up the road, a drama group were performing excerpts from *Twelfth Night* in the back of an old Hillman Imp.

The serious busking would be going on around St Giles and on The Mound outside the Royal Scottish Academy where a small group of South Americans were playing their pipe music from the Andes, struggling to make themselves heard above a jazz ensemble, who in turn were trying to avoid being singed by a bilious flame swallower. 'Hey Jimmy, have ye goat twenty pee furra cup o' tea,' said a red-faced tramp to a man with half a robot's head. Getting no response, save a robotic wave, he staggered off to hustle the young man below the pillars who was putting the finishing touches to a 12-foot chalk version of El Greco's *Saviour of the World*. 'Here – that's guid,' he says. 'Have ye goat the price o' a cuppa tea?'

There were three people in a row, fast asleep, in the Royal Lyceum Theatre. The Kathakali Theatre Company had spent six hours arranging their costumes and carefully painting their faces for an Indian version of *King Lear* and the three took just half an hour to fall asleep. But sleeping during Festival performances is nothing new and is quite permissible, as long as you do not snore, or let your head bounce up and down, or wake up suddenly shouting 'Where's your harmonica, Madeleine?'

The three were woken by a woman coming in late. With Festival shows overlapping like tiles on a slate roof, this is perfectly acceptable. But she was flustered because she had not thought of a really good excuse. The Festival-goer owes it to the ushers to think of something original; they are tired of the old chestnuts about traffic jams and Edinburgh's policemen and the taxi driver who goes to the Assembly Halls in Leith instead of up The Mound. Better to admit you dropped your lipstick in the fish tank and explain you had to change the water before you left. That is the sort of thing that makes their day. Leaving early also demands aplomb: best fake appendicitis and make a run for the exits. Just make sure you know where they are – there is nothing worse than clattering along a row of 17 seats only to find you have to clatter all the way back again to find the right door out.

It is all part of the code for Festival audiences; just as the vogue is now to dress down for the theatre or the concert, unless you are in the really expensive seats when you owe it to the sponsors to drop your choc-ice on something really smart. Peer down from the upper balcony. Most people in the stalls, apart from the odd herbaceous border of summer frocks and a woman with a blue feather boa, look as if they have just come home from work, taken off their clothes, given them to the dog to play with, then put them on again for the evening.

The fear that keeps many people away from hundreds of shows in the first place is the terror of audience participation: of the unsolicited kind (the man sitting beside them in the Usher Hall conducting Mahler's 4th, or the youth with the digital watch which plays *Yankee Doodle* every hour) and the solicited kind (the horror of being picked out of the audience and subjected to ridicule, embarrassment, physical pain or a small plate of custard on their head, the sort of thing that would result in a prosecution in the Sheriff Court at any other time of the year).

The Lyceum audience shut their eyes again; there was a man in a purple mask feigning madness in the middle of the floor. If only that dreary music would go away. Sleep was the only answer.

Oberon looked at his watch, then Oberon looked for his watch – it would be under his pile of clothes somewhere. He would have to get dressed soon, as he was wanting to go to a lunchtime concert at The Queen's Hall before this afternoon's rehearsal. He had a big night planned after the show this evening; they were all going to climb up Arthur's Seat to watch the fireworks explode above the city, then he was going to catch some late night jazz. But at the moment the fireworks were all inside his head. There was a small riot between the beds as Yasmin and her little gang skipped their way through the sleeping figures counting as they went (which wasn't easy as Yasmin had never gone past three). 'Lord,' he thought, 'what fools these mortals be.'

Festival Parade, Princes Street

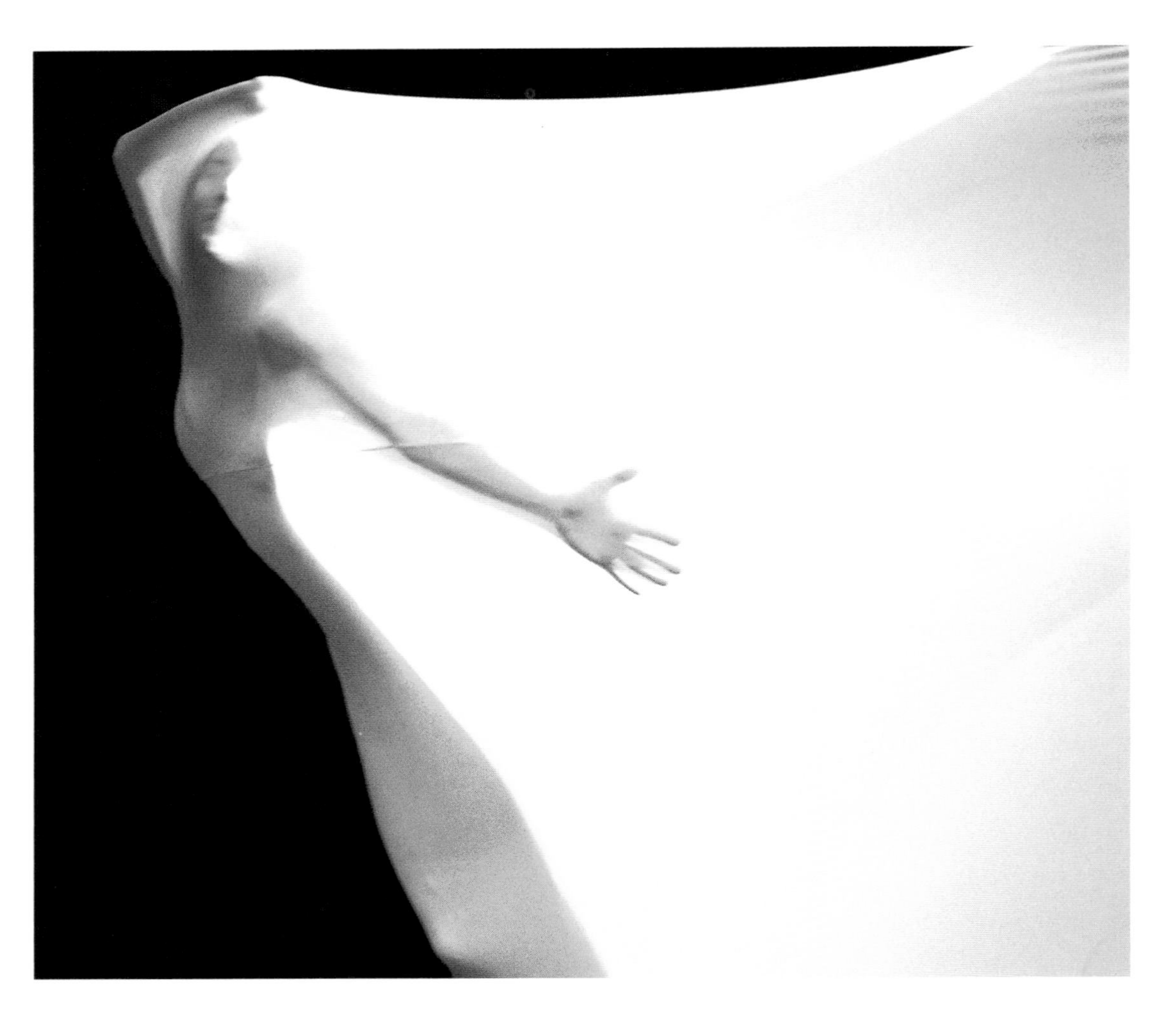

Desires, *Compagnie Philippe Genty (above)*
Rudolph Nuryev in The Overcoat *(left)*
New York Ballet (right)
Busking juggler, The Mound precinct (opposite)

Mandala (above)
Chinese acrobats (right)
Giselle *(below)*
Desert Zoo, *Ban'yu Inryoku (opposite)*

The Cleveland Ballet (top)
Petit Albert, *Comedie de Caen (bottom left)*
Murder in the Cathedral, *National Youth Theatre of Great Britain (bottom right)*

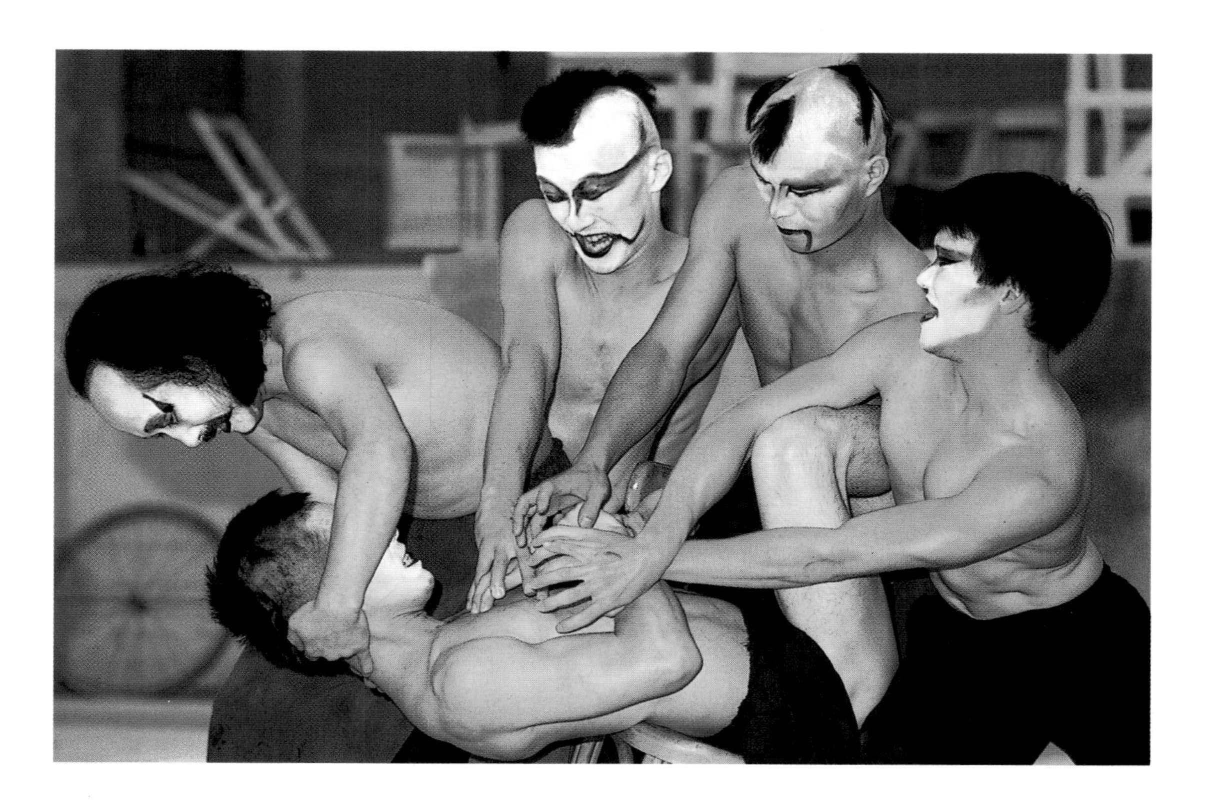

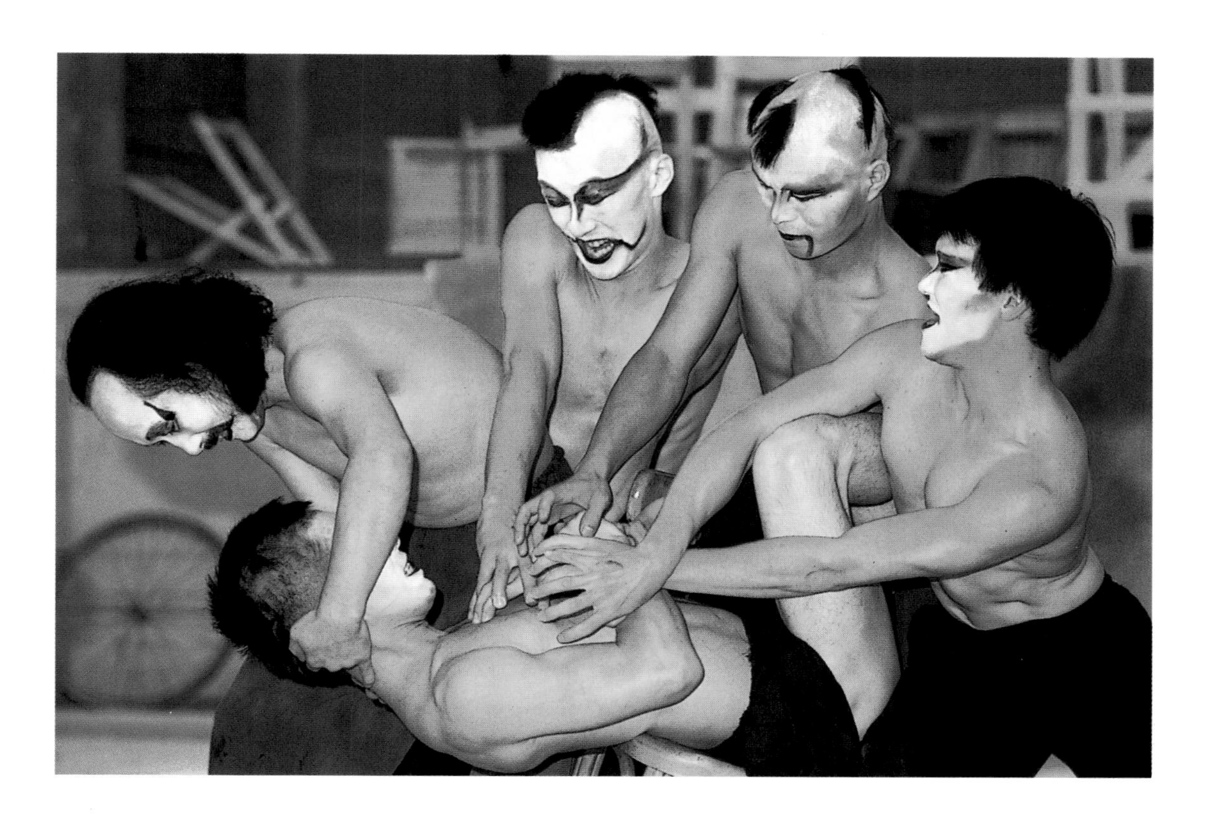

A Chinese Macbeth *(opposite, top)*
Matsuyama Ballet Company (opposite, centre left)
Medea, *The Toho Theatre Company of Japan (opposite, centre right)*
Japanese buskers, Fringe Sunday (opposite, bottom)
Oxford University Player (below)

A Midsummer-night's Dream, *Royal Exchange Theatre Company (bottom left)*
Clown, Festival Parade (bottom centre)
Street painting (bottom right)

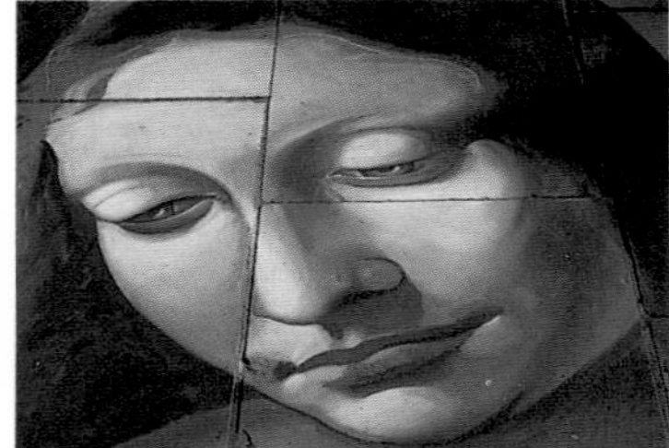

Festival faces (top and bottom)
Market Theatre of Johannesburg (centre)
Slovak National Opera and Ballet (opposite, top)

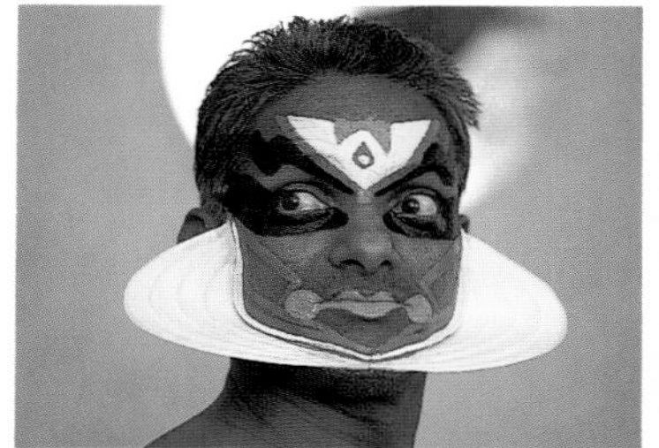

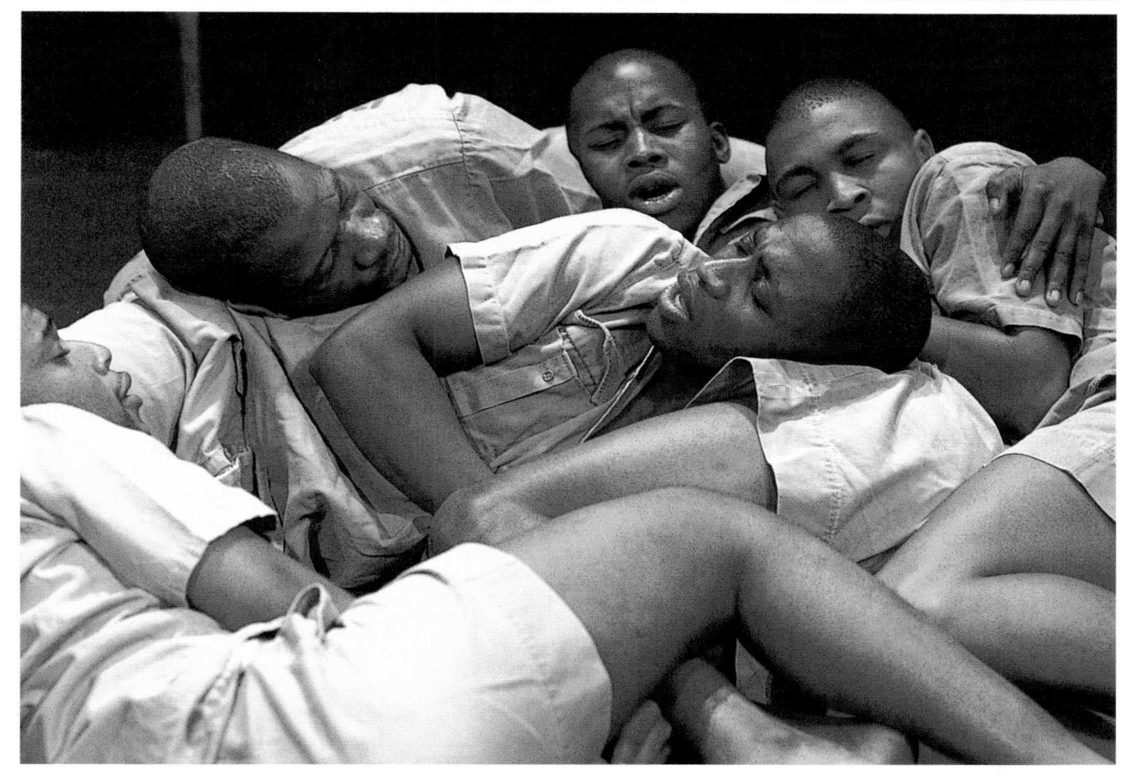

'Colourscape', Fringe Sunday (above)
Mime artist (left)
Official Festival performer (opposite, right)
Buskers (opposite, left)

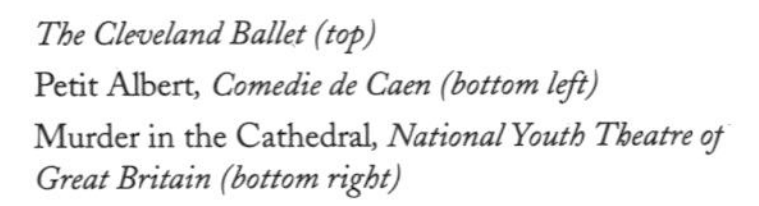

The Cleveland Ballet (top)
Petit Albert, *Comedie de Caen (bottom left)*
Murder in the Cathedral, *National Youth Theatre of Great Britain (bottom right)*

Mephisto, *Slovak National Opera and Ballet(above)*

Preparing for a performance, Rosslyn Chapel vaults (below)

Le Lavoir, *Theatre de la Basoche (right)*

THE SMALLEST THEATRE
IN THE WORLD
BOX
OFFICE
STAGE
DOOR
NEVAL
NEVAL

Festival Pipers
The Smallest Theatre in the World (opposite, top)
Merry-go-round, Fringe Sunday (opposite, bottom)

Le Theatre die la Mie (above)
Archaos (right)
Hamlet, *Oxford Players (opposite, top)*
Street artist (opposite, bottom)

Fringe Sunday (top)
Dimones, *Els Comediantes (centre)*
Ra Ra Zoo (bottom)
Busker (opposite)

Buskers (top and bottom right)
Fringe Sunday (bottom centre)
N-n-nervous Circus performer (bottom left)
Market Theatre of Johannesburg (opposite, top)
Treasure Island, *Festival production (opposite, bottom)*

Dimones, *Els Comediantes (above)*

'Fringe At The Seaside', Portobello (bottom right)

Festival fireworks (bottom left)

Festival fireworks crowd, Princes Street (opposite)

Warriston

4 The Country in the City

They left the halls of residence and, shivering in the cold half-light, pulled their scarves closer to their faces and started to walk down Holyrood Park Road, past the old brewery and down to the roundabout. It was a daft idea, but they had done it every year since they had come to Edinburgh and so had most of their friends (once memorably after an all-night session in the student union). In the distance they could make out other small groups heading in the same direction. The sky began to lighten and they quickened their step as they walked round the front of the Raven's Rock, before starting to climb, feeling their way carefully up the steep channel of The Guttit Haddie and by the side of The Nether Hill. Sandra slipped but Rebecca grabbed her rucksack.

They could see a crowd already on the summit and, fearing they might be late, they almost ran the last part to the top of the hill. But then just as they came panting and blowing towards the summit of Arthur's Seat, picking their way between other groups of students, young families and older people sitting by themselves away from the service, watching the horizon, the first pink rim of the rising sun appeared through the mist and, laughing, they fell on the ground and rubbed their faces with the dew. They did not notice Kenneth creeping up behind them. 'I don't know what you lot think you're doing,' he said cheerfully. 'Waste of time, you'll never have beauty – or grace.' Rebecca dumped him on the turf. 'Happy May Day. See you in tutorial.' And they set off down the hill for an early breakfast, the air already warm on their still-damp faces.

There can hardly be a city in Britain with so much of the countryside within its boundaries. There are hills to climb, woods to walk through, reservoirs to fish, a canal to row on (at least for part of its length) and the seaside to build sand castles on at the edge of the city. Of the hills, Arthur's Seat in Holyrood Park is the most famous, apart perhaps from the Castle Rock itself and few people climb that, other than by the Royal Mile (and if they do try they have to be rescued by the fire brigade). In an old pagan ritual, every May Day people from all over the city rise early to climb its 823 feet and to watch the sunrise. The hill is an integral part of the city; for many years stone was gouged from Salisbury Crags to pave Edinburgh's streets. A 'couchant raglion' according to Charlotte Bronte, Arthur's Seat embraces within its paws two lochs: Dunsapie and St Margaret's. Both were formerly marshlands and now attract wild fowl – ducks, swans and greylag geese – from nearby Duddingston Loch along with Sunday morning walkers from the city. The path which climbs from Holyrood under Salisbury Crags is the most popular route up Arthur's Seat. It is known as the Radical Road and was the idea of Sir Walter Scott and his friends, who employed a group of unemployed weavers from the west of Scotland to clear it, their radical views giving the path its name. Now it is the path itself and the views from it that are famous.

In what was once an old pantry in Hermitage House by the Braid Burn, The Hermits Club were putting the finishing touches to their club room. They had been at it every Saturday for months. 'We drew the pictures first, birds and ponds and trees and things,' said Nick Doyle, sharing a custard cream with his little brother Mark, 'then we painted them and it took quite a long time.' 'And a bit of help from the parents,' said his mother. 'Otherwise we would have had orange blackbirds and purple swans.' He looked down at the thick woollen socks bunched round his ankles. 'And last week we were doing spiders with pipe cleaners and bits of toilet rolls.' A thread spider's web hung down from the door. Inside, they had painted the four walls to represent the changing seasons, the ceiling to represent the sky and the floor to represent their own muddy footprints. The room was heavily perfumed with the natural scent of wood shavings; plaster birds hung down around our heads and leaves were stapled to the trees.

The Hermitage is one of the best walks in the city through a deep and wooded ravine, between Blackford Hill and the Braid Hills, through a forest of sycamores and elms, oaks and beech, and by the side of the narrow banked Braid Burn. There are woodland flowers (wood anemones and wild hyacinths), wildlife (foxes, bats and squirrels), and over ninety species of birds (owls, woodpeckers, cuckoos and herons among them), all along the banks of the burn. All of these were painted (perhaps not quite to scale) on the club room walls. The Hermit Club is run by the District Council's countryside ranger service. During the summer holidays, up to eighty children meet regularly at the old house to play and learn about the countryside within their city. 'They are stunned by the amount of wildlife here,' say the parents. Some days they are divided into Indian tribes - the Sitka, the Tsuga and the Quercus - and they go whooping off into the trees to pick up dead leaves, flowers or twigs for a collage or maybe to make totem poles in the sun. Other times they play Watery Weirdies, dipping jars into the burn to learn about all its waterborne life. As autumn approaches they make bird feeders from empty juice bottles; one boy placed his effort in the middle of the burn 'so the birds can feed while they're having a swim.' The ranger service also leads summer walks through The Hermitage for adults on a wide variety of topics: 'Nature's Pharmacy' (the different uses for plants), 'Fungus' (what to and what not to pick and eat) and 'Poets and Princes' (on the history of the estate which was an old haunt of medieval knights, of Covenanters, and of wealthy 18th-century lairds and their families. Robert Burns was particularly taken with a daughter of the house, Eliza Burnet, of whom he wrote: 'there has not been anything like her in all the combinations of beauty, grace and goodness the great creator has formed since Milton's Eve on the first day of her existence.')

In the club room, one of the little boys fixed a leaf back on its tree. 'We would have got it finished quicker,' he said, 'if it hadn't been for the girls.' And his sister gave him a whack across the ears.

Arthur's Seat

Duddingston (above and opposite)

Hillend (top and bottom left)
Warriston (bottom right)
Blackford Hill (opposite, top)
Ratho (opposite, bottom)

BRIDGE INN

Swanston
Edinburgh from the south (opposite)

Roslin Glen

Roslin Glen

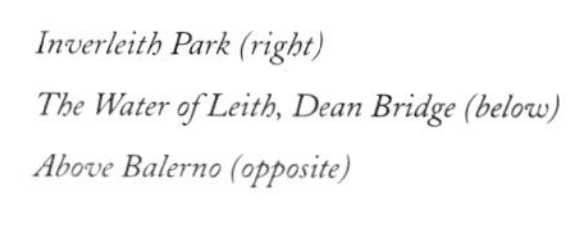

Inverleith Park (right)
The Water of Leith, Dean Bridge (below)
Above Balerno (opposite)

The Water of Leith, Canonmills

The Water of Leith, Dean Village

Edinburgh from the Pentlands (above)
Craigmillar Castle (opposite)
Edinburgh outskirts (pages 114 & 115)

Marchmont Cemetery

5

Graves

George Anderson lay in the sun on his windowsill in the wall of Geyfriars Kirkyard between two dark and faded tombs. It was his usual position, beside the tulips and the daffodils in the windowbox, watching the visitors to the graves, waiting for Kelly and Andrew to come home and feed him. A tourist stopped to take a photograph; but that was nothing unusual – he was used to the way they stared at the windows in the graveyard wall.

Looking from the kitchen at 60 Candlemaker Row it feels as if you are embedded in a headstone. The people walking along the path in the churchyard reading the inscriptions on the murals with their great morbid decorations and ornate coats of arms, often pause just short of the Ray stone (in memory of Adam Ray and 27 members of his family) when they catch sight of the cat on its windowsill. And when they look straight towards you it feels as if you have become part of the very fabric of the graveyard. 'Only a few inches,' wrote Stevenson 'separate the living from the dead.' Sometimes the people in the houses on Candlemaker Row take a short cut, and climb through their windows on their hands and knees. For anyone visiting the graveyard it must be a startling sight.

Graveyards hold the history of a city and for more than two centuries Greyfriars was Edinburgh's archivist. In 1561 it lay outside the town boundary so the Council proposed that the old friary would be a good place to bury the dead, so the air in their town would be all the cleaner. Queen Mary agreed and granted them the friary and its yards. Now it feels as if it is in the very heart of Edinburgh; when you stand between the tombs, the Old Town rises up ahead: the castle on its rock, the tall spire of St John's, the chimneys of the high flats and the tower above the Central Library. And there are people all around you with famous stories; Captain Porteous, who was hanged by an angry mob, James Craig, the architect of the New Town and John Gray – Old Jock – whose dog Bobby proved such a devoted pet. This is where the National Covenant was signed by strict Presbyterians in 1638, an act which triggered a bitter campaign of opposition to Charles I . Over 1200 Covenanters were held prisoner close-by and the 100 or so executed in the Grassmarket are commemorated with a Martyrs' Monument. 'And triumph now in glory with the lamb'.

There used to be an old man, known as The Penny Tramp, who visited the graveyard everyday in his ragged coat, wellington boots and with an old tin helmet on his head. Every morning he would slip a penny under the door of the old bothy and the council workmen would collect it and give it to the church officer for the poor and needy. A little girl in a red duffle coat threw bread for the pigeons by the tomb of Thomas Bannatyne, a cherub ankle deep in dust. An old man lowered himself onto a bench – In memoriam Professor Hans Ferdinand Redlich DPhil MA DMus its carved dedication ran - and opened a pack of sandwiches. A young couple sunbathed between the graves beneath the cherryblossom. Sometimes it is a good place to be alive.

The stones in Greyfriars are not just monuments to the dead they commemorate. They are also monuments to the masons who placed them there, inspired craftsmen who balanced a fear of death with a belief in a glorious resurrection; carved skeletons and skulls vie with angels with their trumpets.

Sometimes a resurrection of a different kind came sooner than expected. Another city trade (of a sort) which flourished in Edinburgh's graveyards was that of the resurrectionists or dog-cart gentlemen or sack' em up men as they were variously known. These robbed graves to offer bodies at a price to the city's anatomists and sometimes in their eagerness to provide the freshest of cadavers they would help someone to an untimely end themselves. Strangely there were two classes of graverobber: the 'Respectable Resurrectionists' who were dedicated to advancing medical progress, and the ordinary thieves who took a more mercenary attitude to their task. It was a cut-throat business. Fierce fighting between rival gangs would often break out over the graves, or members of the public would catch the robbers muddy handed and take exception which just added to the fresh corpses in the yard. Edinburgh tried many methods to protect her graves: traps were set with loaded guns around the graves, lead coffins were made to hold the bodies, and in Greyfriars you can still see the iron bars, or mortsafes, which were meant to keep corpses from prying hands.

There are four watchtowers in the city: at St Cuthbert's, New Calton, Preston Street and Duddingston. They were built in the 1820s when bodysnatching reached its peak and were manned by guards who were employed by the family and friends of the deceased to watch over their recently buried bodies. If they fell asleep on duty they were fined £5 for their laziness, and if a corpse was actually stolen while they watched, they were fined £10 for their stupidity.

St Cuthbert's can be an eerie place. It was being used as a burial ground as early as the 12th century and it still seems almost like a village churchyard, in its dip below the main drag south of Princes Street. Many of the city's down-and-outs – Cowboy and Rosie Redface to name but two – now sleep among the graves, under the church steps, in the Gothic vaulted tomb of Baron Gordon and in the burial ground of the Reverend David Dickson, 'one of the ministers of this parish'. They leave notes for one another among the stones arranging to rendezvous at Greyfriars or Calton on the hill.

In her studio above St Cuthbert's Kirkyard, Sally Smith finishes a sculpture of a human head. 'It can be a lonely place to work,' she says 'with the living on one side and the dead on the other.' The old watch-tower can be cold – 'the clay often freezes and becomes brittle' – and it is not a good place to work at night.

There is still a watchtower above the terraces of New Calton cemetery, though it has not yet been renovated like the studio at St Cuthbert's. Many of the graves which were disturbed in Old Calton were moved here in 1815 when Regent's Bridge was built to join Princes Street to Calton Hill. Old Calton cemetery is the most visible in the centre of the city from where Robert Adam's circular tomb for the philosopher David Hume and the tall needle erected in honour of the political reformers of 1793 blend in with the other classical pieces on the hill. It also provides a fine view in the other direction across the southern sections of the Old Town.

The business of bodysnatching in Edinburgh was

finally laid to rest in 1832 when corpses could legally be made available to doctors. The case which finally acted as a catalyst to legislation was that of the infamous duo, William Burke and William Hare. They were not graverobbers; they found other ways to supply bodies to the city's anatomists and the public outcry when they were caught was enough to see that the law was changed. Now visitors can rest in peace – those who look out over the graveyard have more peaceful intentions. On his windowsill, George Anderson stretched out in the sun, yawned licked his paws and curled himself back to sleep.

Greyfriars Kirkyard

Greyfriars Kirkyard (above)
Dean Cemetery (opposite)

DAVID OCTAVIUS

Inveresk Cemetery (left and top right, and opposite, bottom)
Warriston Cemetery (bottom right)
Holyrood Abbey (opposite, top)

SANS PEUR JE PENS

EMANCIPATION
SERGEANT MAJOR JOHN MCEWAN
WILLIAM L. DUFF
ROBERT STEEDMAN
JAMES WILKIE
TO PRESERVE
THE JEWEL OF LIBERTY
IN THE FRAMEWORK OF
FREEDOM
IN MEMORY OF SCOTTISH-AMERICAN SOLDIERS

Calton Cemetery (top)

Marchmont Cemetery (bottom)

Monument to Scottish Americans who died in the American Civil War, Old Calton Cemetery (opposite)

Clovenstone

6

Wester Hailes

Aisha Mohammed dipped her paintbrush into the wax, wiped it gently against the side of the pan then traced the delicate outline of an autumn leaf. 'We came here eight and a half years ago.' She stepped back to inspect her work – a silk banner for International Women's Day – and smoothed her jacket down over her satin kameez. 'We were desperate to get out of Wester Hailes at first. But not now, not just for the sake of it; there really are worse places to live.' And she began to colour the leaf with orange dye, spreading the colour in circles with the tip of her finger. 'We moved here from Huddersfield, although my parents originally came from Faisalabad in Pakistan. Now I think of myself as Scottish,' she said. 'My sisters and I always speak English together even here at the group. But when the older Asian women meet here every Friday, they just gossip in Punjabi.'

Aisha says she is lucky. She lives in a three-storey block in Wester Hailes, away from the hated high-rises. 'It is a four-bedroomed apartment and there are eight of us; my parents, two brothers and my sisters, Zahida, Shahida and Noreen'. Every day she travels to Stirling were she is studying accountancy at the university: 'I don't think I would've been allowed to stay in the student accommodation.'

The tape of bhangra music suddenly stops as Zahida winds it on to her favourite track. There are many Muslims in Wester Hailes. 'We find it hard to go all the way to the mosque in Edinburgh. We are all busy and it's too far away. But we are meant to pray five times a day and we always observe Ramadan, getting up at half past three in the morning for our first meal, and then we have nothing until later in the evening.'

Her voice is small and Scottish, her eyes bright under their heavy, long-lashed lids. 'It can be difficult to live in Wester Hailes. A lot of kids, even really wee kids, shout racial abuse at you when you go out to the shops. Last week as we were leaving here to walk to the car, a couple of boys said really nasty things, not straight out, but under their breath.' She cocked her head, looking at her painting. 'But that's not just Wester Hailes. My uncle even has problems in Corstorphine. Racists are everywhere.'

The door is locked from the inside. Beyond the dark edges of the park, the houses form a circle like a wagon train, dogs bark under the street lights, there is the sound of glass breaking somewhere beyond the bridge. The girls hurry out towards their car.

Clovestone is one of the communities which make up Wester Hailes; a sprawling urban development built in the 1960s on the edge of Edinburgh. At that time, the city' s housing list was stretched far beyond any reasonable limit; family housing was overcrowded, there was no accommodation for young people ready to leave home or for young families starting life together. Something had to be done and that something, it was decided, would be to create a new city suburb in the west. At first they planned mostly low-rise developments, three- or four-storey flats, jointed to a park at Hailes Quarry by a long pedestrian walkway, 'like a 20th-century Royal Mile' according to the Council. But building regulations forced the city to build fewer, and by necessity, higher flats further apart. Now one-third of all households are in damp, high-rise blocks in the middle of a bleak environment, with no gardens, few shops and hardly any play areas for children, surrounded by car parks which are seldom used and joined by gloomy vandalised subways. 'When you move into a multi-storey block of flats you will realise that there are several features which are unique to high-rise living,' says the tenants' handbook. Looking down on the pale grey concrete wedges, they look like giant pieces from some hopeless board game – a loser's Monopoly.

Lisa and Kate expect to sell their bong within a week. It is a huge one, five feet high at least, all carved wood and inlaid brass, with four long pipes snaking down from its neck. 'There is a big market for anything drug-related here,' says Lisa as she lights a cigarette. 'They will always find the money for it somehow if they want it.' The girls have set up shop in the Wester Hailes Centre, selling hippy pipes and incense sticks, plaster skulls wrapped in scarves and packs of lurid tarot cards. 'The nastiest stuff always sells well.' There is a strong smell of incense all around us; a Pink Floyd tape plays loudly in the corner and one or two grubby children hang around the doorway; a young man with a red pocked face and carrying a cane, hobbles in to borrow a joss stick to clean his pipe. It is a depressing place. 'People stay in the centre all day long. At least it is warm and it saves them money on heating their homes. But you see some terrible things here.'

They have lost of a lot of their stock – 'no one comes in for ages, then fifteen kids come in all at once and something goes missing' – and they do not expect to be in business very long. 'I don't think I could stand it,' says Kate, shaping a piece of clay into a little red toadstool. Across the corridor, the butcher stares at them as he saws a string of sausages in front of an old black and white poster of Princes Street.

But there are two sides of Wester Hailes. 'The people who complain,' says Fiona Glasgow, behind her desk in the WHOT shop in the centre, 'are the people who aren't doing anything for the community. I feel really lucky to have been brought up in Wester Hailes; most of my education has come from people in the community. It's true a lot of planning mistakes were made when they built this place, but we are trying to do something about it.' WHOT stands for the Wester Hailes Opportunities Trust which offers local people an opportunity to improve their lot through courses, finding regular employment, training, or social enterprise or community work; it also organises a career service, group meetings and skills workshops. It is primarily run by the local residents, like several other organisations initiated by the community to help itself: good neighbour schemes, festival groups, arts and leisure enterprises, and social clubs. The best hope for Wester Hailes has always rested with the spirit and resources of its people.

In front of the shopping centre, the mural group are painting *Education*: four heads filled with images of learning. They change the mural four times a year. 'It's difficult to do something more permanent because of the environment,' says Kathy Jones. An old man with a shopping trolley stops to stare. 'Our murals are all about life in Wester Hailes' – she moves four-year-old Merlin out of the way by his braces – 'because we are all from Wester Hailes and anyway we find it hard to agree on national issues'.

By the toddlers' pool in the Wester Hailes Education Centre, a little girl climbs into a giant red toadstool and slides back down into the water. Her granny, 68 today, is in the big pool doing the Gay Gordons with Mrs Burns. Every Tuesday they meet for their over-50s fitness sessions, climbing into their one-piece bathing suits, standing up to their waists by the shallow end, dancing their hearts out.

It is hard not to feel optimism and despair in equal measure walking around Wester Hailes. Despair because of the task ahead to transform the developer's nightmare into a decent place to live, optimism because of the feeling of a caring community which radiates from the people like Aisha, Fiona, Kathy and the ladies in the pool. 'Wester Hailes – Full of Potential' goes the jingle. You could say that about any deprived area of the city but it seems particularly true when you meet some of the people in this bleak outpost on the west of Edinburgh.

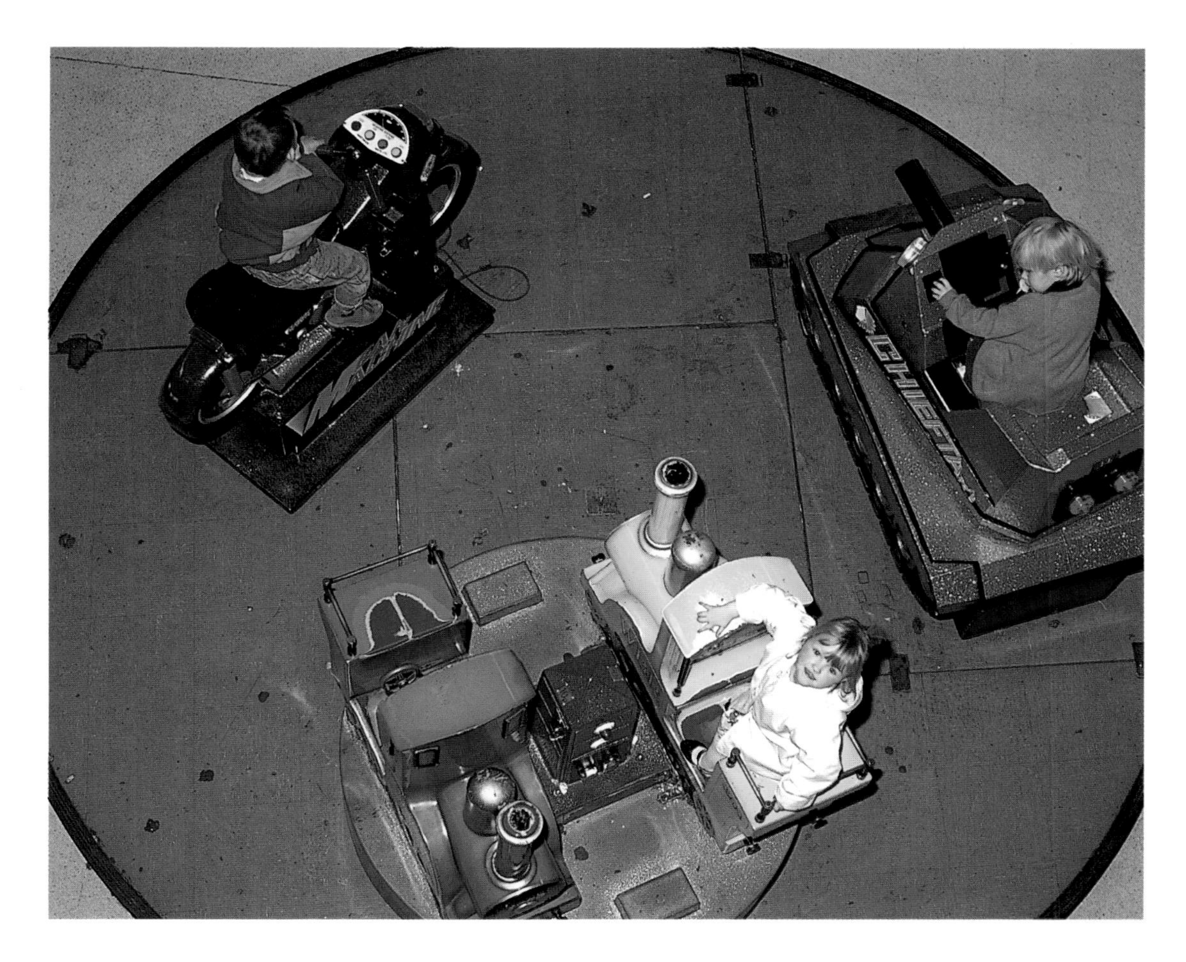

Wester Hailes Education Centre (top left and bottom right)
Hailesland (top right and bottom left)

ORA
NGE
JUICE

Westburn (top and bottom left)

Hailesland (centre)

Clovenstone (bottom right and opposite, top)

Wester Hailes Community Play Hut (opposite, bottom right)

Underpass, Wester Hailes Shopping Centre (above)
Wester Hailes Community Play Hut (below)

EMERGENCY EXIT
PLEASE KEEP A
SAFE DISTANCE!
EMERGENCY EXIT
BREAK GLASS
E440 JSG
WESTER
HAILES
Full of Potential!

Granton

7

Edinburgh's Coast

They were combing the beach at Portobello. A tractor, all smoke signals and smut, was dragging a rake behind itself, scraping the sands, picking out nits, looking for litter lice. Where the sand was soft, its wheels spun as slowly as a windmill in Spain. The tide had gone east, leaving a two-tone shore, butterscotch and chocolate brown. A young couple lay stretched out above the tide mark, baking on their towels, while the tractor dragged the sand around them. It was hot. In the distance the sea disappeared into a wet grey haze. Two butterflies surrounded a bright blue bench in a hurry. On the next bench a Greek chorus, four men with pink skulls, whisps of white hair and comfortable brown shoes, shook their heads in the heat.

It was early yet. People were waiting to see if the day was really this warm before heading towards the shore. Not that many would come. Edinburgh uses its seaside like a schoolboy uses his handkerchief – reluctantly. People spend years in the city without walking down to the sea; for them the seaside is somewhere else in another country. Puerto Bello.

I walked along the salmon pink esplanade from Joppa, the wide footpath as smooth as an operating table, uncontaminated at least by people. This was where they built the fashionable villas in the 19th century and it was to the Joppa end of the beach that social aspirants would drift on their day trips from the city. Portobello reached the zenith of its popularity at the beginning of the 20th century when trams and trains would empty crowds onto Bath Street, into the Marine Gardens and towards the Pier, where Edinburgh stretched 1250 feet further into the sea.

On their bench by the dilapidated water sports club, near the sandstone baths and its first-floor cafe (No need to Swim, Just come in), the Greek chorus spun their home-style philosophies. 'There's some are born moaning,' they said. 'And they'll be moaning 'til they're under the turf. It's just human nature.' And seagulls paddled across the shore.

By Beach Lane, children were singing, yelling at the top of their voices 'I can sing a rain-bow' to drown out the screams of the machines in the empty arcades. Next door, behind one of the arcades and its mock medieval façade, sat a strange octagonal castellated tower built in 1785 as a summer house, a flight of fantasy oddly in keeping with the tasteless trappings of the Porty fun shows.

Beyond the Tides Inn, the sand was smudged and darker, closely packed and pocked with rocks, the beach infinitely less inviting; there, without interruption, the esplanade psychologically became no more than a broad straight path beside the sea. On the other side, football pitches now lay where people once used to swim in a huge outdoor swimming pool, in its time one of the most modern in Europe with a championship diving pool, slides and one of the first electric wave-making machines to lick the ears of British bathers.

Beyond the yelping of the strays in the cat-and-dog home, the path narrowed as it followed an old railway line past the industrial warehouses of Seafield and on down to the port of Leith. On the edge of Leith, down by the docks, the architecture is a strange mixture of the domestic and the industrial. Although the process of gentrification has slowed after the initial burst of enthusiasm in the 1980s, there still seem to be plenty of people eager to live amongst the dust and within sight of the debris from one of Scotland's busiest ports. For although the nature of many of the shipments has changed over the years, Leith docks are now busier than ever, fielding cargoes of coal, grain, oil pipes and animal feed and providing a berth for 36 cruise ships every year.

Much is still made of the difference between the people of Edinburgh and Leith but here the packs are shuffled. Outside the Waterfront Wine Bar, by Rennie's Lock, the young business set and the Nouveau Leithers sit drinking in the sun while the staff squeeze between the tables with plates of *crevettes* and *leeks en croûte* and another bottle of creamy yellow Chardonnay.

Not far away, on the other side of the huge Imperial dry dock, there is an old tower in the middle of a pipe field. Few people know it is there. It is an old Martello tower, half-buried by the process of land reclamation, built in 1809 as part of a system of defences to repel Napoleon Bonaparte. I squeezed through the narrow entrance and into a dark chamber half-filled with water and spiked with knitting needle-thin stalactites. Old worn steps led up to the ramparts and from there the docks lay spread out around me: container ships at anchor, cranes idling with their hands up, a three-masted schooner, the *Pride of Baltimore*, flying the Stars and Stripes. Most of the ground around me was landfill although it is said that when the tower was first built, its base, Mussel Cape Rock, was half a mile out at sea.

On Constitution Street, Grampian House and Cairngorm House, those twin peaks of the architects' art of the early 1960s, sat like two sad grey monoliths. Underneath Grampian, a small crowd had gathered to watch as smoke poured out of the 16th floor. 'That's J wing,' said a woman with her hands against her hips. 'I wish it had been mine then I might have got rehoused quicker. They're all due to come down soon.' And a man in a white coat went to get a pie to eat while he watched, as the first sirens sounded somewhere out of sight around the bend.

Newhaven Harbour looks like a sheep pen, herding its small flock of pleasure craft and a pair of lobster boats between its mossy flanks. Four boys were fishing at its mouth while above them, a shirtless figure sat slumped in the sun against the half-sized lighthouse. Sitting on a row of fishboxes, their backs against warm rubbed stone, another Greek chorus (pink scalps, tufts of white hair, comfortable brown shoes) watched as the world passed them by.

Newhaven was as independent of Edinburgh in its time as Leith. It was a royal shipbuilding yard and later a great herring port, famous for the fishwives who used to roll through the streets of Edinburgh in traditional costume with their baskets of fish. In the Peacock Inn beside the harbour, there is a collection of portraits of Bow Tows (as the Newhaven natives were known) taken in 1843 by the pioneering photographers Hill and Adamson. They look like the cast of a Benjamin Britten opera. For many years Newhaven was also the oyster capital of Scotland as the local fishermen shaved the scalp beds of the Forth. At its height the industry would send out 30 million oysters a year. Now the port is quiet, the oysters have gone, the shipbuilding is finished and most of the fishermen that are left sail from Port Seton.

Newhaven also used to have a busy ferry service, so busy in fact that a new pier, the Chain Pier, was built in 1821 to serve the steam packets sailing between the port and Queensferry, Grangemouth and Alloa. Understandably, the Bow Tows were dismayed when eventually they lost the business to the new harbour at 'Godless Granton'. And there is a ferry service again at Granton after a 30-year hiatus. The 80-ton *Spirit of Fife* sails every day between the harbour and the Kingdom, carrying commuters from Burntisland in the morning and home from work in the evening and tourists under the Forth Bridges every afternoon. But apart from that there is little activity at Granton, besides the fleet of pleasure boats and on the odd occasion when the tide is against the Port Seton fishing boats and they call in for a night.

It is a long haul walking the Granton coast beside the gas works and between bland industrial units before the wide sweep of green parkland which leads to Cramond, Edinburgh's Roman village. There was a warm, salty smell of seaweed in the air, an old man on his bicycle wobbled along a broad avenue of trees, and in the distance the finger tips of the Forth's bridges appeared through the haze.

As I walked towards the village, waves lapped at the top of the causeway to Cramond Island. Hardly a month goes by without a gang of children crossing to play on the 19-acre island, only to find themselves stranded by the tide rushing back. Nearby, a group of people had lit a bonfire on the shore and were trying to burn sausages on a rusty rack.

It was quiet. A flock of swans floated across the mouth of the River Almond straightening their necks, staring down through their own reflections. The whitewashed houses at the foot of the village radiated the afternoon heat like furnace doors. And at the short crossing over the River Almond to Dalmeny Woods, one of the shortest ferry routes in Scotland, Cramond's own gondolier, Bob Graham, dipped a single oar into the liquid gold and paddled his skiff across the river.

That is the way to leave Edinburgh. Stand on the riverside at Cramond, shout for the boat and don't stop walking until you have crossed the bridge to Fife.

Leith sunset

Portobello

FUNFAIR

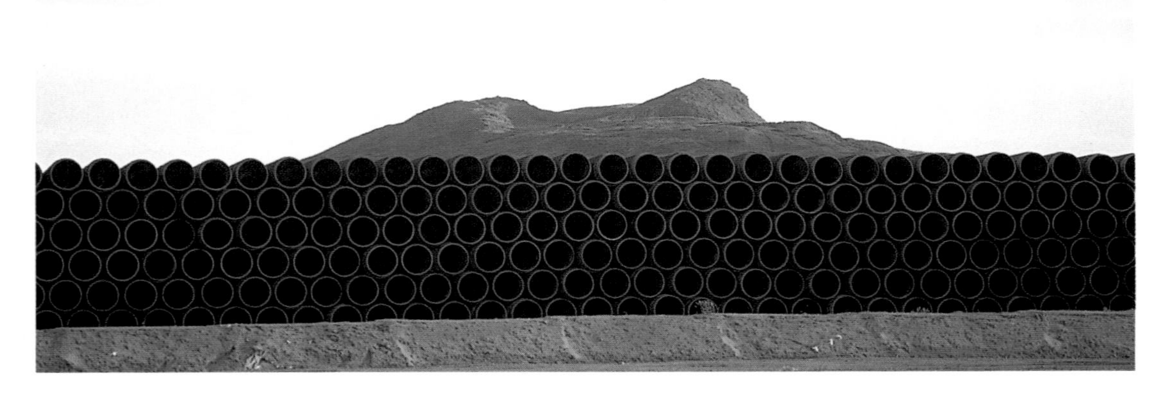

Leith docks (above and opposite , bottom
Oil tankers on the Firth of Forth (opposite, top)

Leith

Restaurant & Bar
OCEAN MIST
Leith

ALL
WISE
LADIES
COLLECT
BLUE
COUPONS
CHARLOTTE STREET

1864

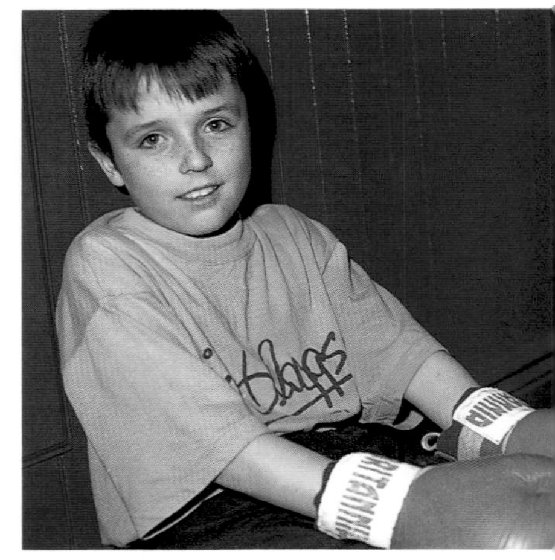

Victoria Boxing Club, Leith
(top and bottom right)
Leith (bottom left and opposite)

SHOPPING CENTRE

Granton (below)
Newhaven (opposite)

Granton (above and opposite)

Cramond

DANGER
WATER COVERS
CAUSEWAY
AT HIGH TIDE

Dalmeny House

Cramond

The Forth Bridge

The Forth Road Bridge (top and bottom left)
South Queensferry (bottom right)

The Forth Road Bridge (above)
Centenary fireworks, Forth Bridge (opposite)

I would like to thank the many individuals and organisations who helped me in the course of taking photographs for this book, particularly the Wester Hailes Partnership, Commpress Ltd, the Mount Royal Hotel, and Edinburgh District Council Department of Recreation.

MARIUS ALEXANDER